Sum
OI

White Fragility
Robin DiAngelo

Conversation Starters

By Paul Adams
Book Habits

Bonus Downloads
Get Free Books with *__Any Purchase__* of Conversation Starters!

Every purchase comes with a FREE download!

Add spice to any conversation
Never run out of things to say
Spend time with those you love

Get it Now

or Click Here.

Scan Your Phone

Tips for Using Conversation Starters:

EVERY GOOD BOOK CONTAINS A WORLD FAR DEEPER THAN the surface of its pages. Questions herein are designed to bring us beneath the surface of the page and invite us into the world that lives on. These questions can be used to:

- Foster a deeper understanding of the book
- Promote an atmosphere of discussion for groups
- Assist in the study of the book, either individually or corporately
- Explore unseen realms of the book as never seen before

Table of Contents

Introducing *White Fragility*

Robin DiAngelo authored the slim yet penetrating book *White Fragility: Why It's So Hard for White People to Talk About Racism.* In this new book, she makes a very provocative statement: "I am white and addressing a common white dynamic. I am mainly writing to a white audience; when I use the terms us and we I am referring to the white collective." She beckons her fellow white people to their unjust marginalization. Her message is simple to her fellow white people: Your sensitivity is 'an obstacle to progress.'

Robin DiAngelo introduces us to the phrase 'white fragility.' She defines this phrase as "a state in which even a minimum amount of racial stress becomes intolerable, triggering a range of defensive moves."

She described the varied reactions of many white people whom she meets in her trainings. Their offices sends them to these trainings and they show up defensive and they stay defensive. They push back against all exercises and ideas. They do not deny the existence of racism and its horrible effects however, they refuse to concede that they themselves might have racism in their lives.

She shares stories that in her trainings, most white participants were once challenged for their evasiveness by fellow workers who were not white. No matter the manner of response, these people claim that they were being attacked and were treated "as white" rather than a unique individual who they know they are. They would tune out, pout, nitpick and even blurt awkward jokes. DiAngelo says that one white woman left the training when she was challenged to reconsider a statement she said. The friends of this woman insisted that it almost triggered a heart attack for the lady.

The advice that DiAngelo has for her readers is fairly straightforward yet not that easy to act on. She advocates her fellow white people to abandon their ideas of racism as a matter of the individuals being moral or immoral, good or bad. She says that white people need to accept that they have unconscious investments in whiteness that they may not fully understand. They should seek out the perspectives of different people of color, seek to embrace the discomfort it may produce and avoid confusing discomfort with literal danger. They should intentionally start uncomfortable conversations with their friends and family. Breathing slowly will help. Perhaps the most important of all is remember that these things should be done not for the people of color, rather do it for ourselves. Do it in the spirit of honesty and truth. DiAngelo admonishes that if only white people would truly do what they need to do to shed their fragility, their interpersonal relationships will change and so will their institutions. The major obstacle is that people do not like the feeling of being uncomfortable.

DiAngelo's book is "unapologetically rooted in identity politics." Racial identity is assigned by people whose race is dominant in a certain community. For multiracial people, racial identity is further complicated by their parents' racial identity and the racial demographics of the community where they were raised. The term "passing" also has its dynamics as being perceived as white. This also shapes the identity of a multiracial person. This passing will grant him or her the rewards given by the society for whiteness. However, people who are born with mixed racial heritage may pass as white but will also experience a feeling of isolation and resentment from the people who cannot pass. Multiracial people may not ever be seen as "real" people of any color.

World Trust President Shakti Butler says that she "find[s] hope in this book because of its potential to disrupt the patterns and relationships that have emerged out of long-standing colonial principles and beliefs." *My Grandmother's Hands and Rock the Boat* author Resmaa Menakem says that *White Fragility* "loosens the bonds of white supremacy and binds us back together as human beings." *Courageous Conversations About Race* author Glenn E. Singleton says that DiAngelo "invites white progressives to have a courageous conversation about their culture of complicity." *Beyond Inclusion, Beyond Empowerment* author Leticia Nieto says that DiAngelo "demonstrates an all-too-rare ability to enter the racial conversation with complexity, nuance, and deep respect." *Publishers Weekly* says that this book is "thoughtful, instructive, and comprehensive . . . impressive in its scope and complexity." *Shelf Awareness* says that the book *White Fragility* should be read by everyone and most who read this book "will be inspired to search themselves and interrupt their contributions to racism."

Discussion Questions

"Get Ready to Enter a New World"

Tip: Begin with questions dealing with broader issues to ensure ample time for quality discussions. Read through all discussion questions before engaging.

~~~

question 1

In the book, DiAngelo begins with this statement: "I am white and addressing a common white dynamic." Who are her audience? What is the white collective?

~~~

~~~

question 2

DiAngelo beckons her fellow white people to their unjust marginalization. Her message is their sensitivity is 'an obstacle to progress.' How does racial sensitivity become an obstacle to progress?

~~~

question 3

Robin DiAngelo recognizes that there is racial sensitivity among white people like her. She introduces the phrase 'white fragility.' What is white fragility?

~ ~ ~

question 4

In her years of training people, DiAngelo describes the varied reactions of many white people whom their offices sends. They show up defensive and they stay defensive. How do white people become defensive? Describe the typical reactions in DiAngelo's trainings?

~~~

question 5

DiAngelo says that white people do not deny the existence of racism and its horrible effects. However, they refuse to concede that they themselves might have racism in their lives. Why do white people think that racism is a far subject in their lives?

~~~

question 6

DiAngelo shares that in her trainings, most white participants were once challenged for their evasiveness by fellow workers who were not white. How do people of color challenge whites about their evasiveness?

~~~

~~~

question 7

No matter the manner of response, many white people claim that they were being attacked and were treated "as white" rather than a unique individual who they know they are. How are people treated "as white"?

~~~

question 8

DiAngelo advocates her fellow white people to abandon their ideas of racism as a matter of the individuals being moral or immoral, good or bad. How do white people equate racism with morality?

~~~

question 9

DiAngelo says that white people need to accept that they have unconscious investments in whiteness that they may not fully understand. What are the usual unconscious investments in whiteness? Why do they need to accept their existence?

~~~

~~~

question 10

DiAngelo says that whites should seek to embrace the discomfort that they may feel and avoid confusing discomfort with literal danger. How will white people differentiate discomfort from real danger?

~~~

question 11

The most important of all, according to DiAngelo, is to remember that whites should do things not for the people of color, rather do it for ourselves. Why is it important to have this perspective? What is the danger if whites do it for people of color?

~~~

question 12

DiAngelo admonishes that if white people would truly shed their fragility, their interpersonal relationships will change and so will their institutions. How will institutions change when fragility is removed?

~~~

question 13

DiAngelo's book *White Fragility* is "unapologetically rooted in identity politics." Racial identity is assigned by people whose race is dominant in a certain community. What is identity politics? How does it affect communities with mixed races?

question 14

The term "passing" has its dynamics as being perceived as white. This also shapes the identity of a multiracial person. What is "passing"? How does a multiracial person "pass" as white?

question 15

When people who are born with mixed racial heritage pass as white, they experience benefits and also setbacks. What are the setbacks that people of color who "pass" experience?

~~~

question 16

World Trust President Shakti Butler says that she "find[s] hope in this book because of its potential to disrupt the patterns and relationships that have emerged out of long-standing colonial principles and beliefs." What are the patterns that have emerged from colonialism?

~~~

question 17

My Grandmother's Hands and Rock the Boat author Resmaa Menakem says that *White Fragility* "loosens the bonds of white supremacy and binds us back together as human beings." What is white supremacy? How does DiAngelo's book loosen its bonds?

question 18

Courageous Conversations About Race author Glenn E. Singleton says that DiAngelo "invites white progressives to have a courageous conversation about their culture of complicity." Describe the current culture of complicity. How can white progressives make a difference?

~ ~ ~

question 19

Beyond Inclusion, Beyond Empowerment author Leticia Nieto says that DiAngelo "demonstrates an all-too-rare ability to enter the racial conversation with complexity, nuance, and deep respect." How does DiAngelo exhibit respect about a very controversial topic?

~ ~ ~

~~~

question 20

The New Yorker says that *White Fragility* is a "irrefutable exposure of racism in thought and action, and its call for humility and vigilance." How does the book *White Fragility* evoke humility and vigilance among its readers?

~~~

Introducing the Author

Robin DiAngelo is the author of three books including the *New York Times* best-selling book *White Fragility: Why It's So Hard for White People to Talk About Racism.* DiAngelo shares that she grew up poor. She admits that she felt class oppression while growing up. It was very visible to her but her race privilege has not. She set on a quest to learn how her race has shaped her life. She sought to gain a deeper insight on race and how her other group locations have led her to collude with racism. In doing so, she was able to address the depth of how her multiple locations function together to hold racism in place.

Now, she holds the distinction that she grew up poor and white. However her experience of poverty would've been different if she were not white.

Robin DiAngelo attended Seattle University. From here she earned her bachelor's degree in History and Sociology. She graduated Valedictorian of her class. Thereafter, DiAngelo pursued a Master's Degree in Education from University of Washington. In 2004, DiAngelo graduated with a Doctor of Philosophy degree in Critical Multicultural Education and Whiteness Studies from University of Washington. DiAngelo's doctoral dissertation is entitled "Whiteness in racial dialogue: a discourse analysis".

The committee that received her doctoral dissertation was chaired by Professor James Banks. In 2007, DiAngelo joined the faculty of Westfield State University. In 2014, she was given the position as a tenured professor of Multicultural Education. She has taught courses on Inter-group Dialogue Facilitation, Multicultural Teaching, Anti-Racist Education and Cultural Diversity & Social Justice. DiAngelo's area of research and expertise is Whiteness Studies and Critical Discourse Analysis. She explains how Whiteness is present and further reproduced in everyday narratives. In 2015, she resigned from her position at Westfield University. She has since taught as a part-time professor at the School of Social Work in University of Washington.

While teaching at the University of Washington's School of Social Work, DiAngelo received the Student's Choice Award for Educator of the Year twice.

She is currently pursuing a full-time writing career. Her work and research on *White Fragility* has been recognized and featured in different media publications like *Slate, NPR, Salon, the Atlantic, Alternet, The Seattle Times* and *The New York Times*. Her book was published by Beacon Press in 2018.

For over 20 years, DiAngelo has been a consultant and trainer on issues of racial and social justice. She was appointed by the City of Seattle to co-design the Race and Social Justice Initiative Anti-Racism training together with Darlene Flynn. She has worked with a number of organizations that include non-profit, private, and governmental organizations. As of February 2017, DiAngelo has also served as the director of Equity for Sound Generations in Seattle, Washington.

DiAngelo is widely known as the one who coined the term "white fragility". She first used the term in a peer-reviewed paper she write in 2011. This term was used in contrast to the jargon "people of color." DiAngelo defined white fragility as "a state in which even a minimum amount of racial stress becomes intolerable, triggering a range of defensive moves." She regularly conducts workshops and seminars on the topic. In 2012, DiAngelo wrote *What Does it Mean to be White?: Developing White*

Racial Literacy. This was followed by her book *Is Everyone Really Equal?: An Introduction to Key Concepts in Social Justice Education.* This was published in 2017 as part of Multicultural Education Series. In 2018, she wrote her bestselling book *White Fragility: Why It's So Hard for White People to Talk about Racism.*

Fireside Questions

"What would you do?"

Tip: These questions can be a fun exercise as it spurs creativity among the readers by allowing alternate scene endings and "if this was you" questions.

~~~

question 21

Robin DiAngelo says that she grew up poor and white. However her experience of poverty would've been different if she were not white. How are the experiences of poor white people different from that of poor people of color?

~~~

question 22

DiAngelo sought to gain a deeper insight on race and how her other group locations have led her to collude with racism. How did DiAngelo's multiple locations hold together racism in place?

question 23

DiAngelo's doctoral dissertation is entitled "Whiteness in racial dialogue: a discourse analysis". How does whiteness appear in everyday dialogues? How can dialogues be described as racial?

question 24

DiAngelo is widely known as the one who coined the term "white fragility". She first used the term in a peer-reviewed paper she write in 2011. What is white fragility? How is this concept visible in everyday life?

question 25

For over 20 years, DiAngelo has been a consultant and trainer on issues of racial and social justice. Corporations and organizations send their personnel to learn about mixed-race workplaces. How will institutions change if white fragility will be removed?

~ ~ ~

question 26

People who are born with mixed racial heritage may pass as white but will also experience a feeling of isolation and resentment from the people who cannot pass. If you were mixed race and you "passed,"how will you deal with the resentment from your own people?

~ ~ ~

question 27

"Passing" shapes the identity of a multiracial person. This passing will grant him or her the rewards given by the society for whiteness. If you were an immigrant, will you seek to "pass" as white to get all the privileges? Or will you be content with the privileges you have of being in America?

~ ~ ~

question 28

The major obstacle in thriving multicultural corporations and organizations is that people do not like the feeling of being uncomfortable. If you were the supervisor of a team that has different races, how will you handle racial conflicts among them?

question 29

DiAngelo admonishes that if only white people would shed their fragility, their interpersonal relationships will change and so will their institutions. If you were a person of mixed heritage and you were given a high position in your company, how will you manage your team if they have racial presumptions about you?

~ ~ ~

~ ~ ~

question 30

Most white people say that they were once challenged for their evasiveness by fellow workers who were not white. They claim that they were being attacked and were treated "as white" rather than a unique individual who they know they are. If you were white, would you also receive the treatment of your fellow workers as an attack? Why or why not?

~ ~ ~

Quiz Questions

"Ready to Announce the Winners?"

Tip: Create a leaderboard and track scores to see who gets the most correct answers. Winners required. Prizes optional.

quiz question 1

One term presented by DiAngelo has its dynamics as being perceived as white. This shapes the identity of a multiracial person and will grant him the rewards given by the society for whiteness. What is this term?

quiz question 2

DiAngelo coined the phrase that means "a state in which even a minimum amount of racial stress becomes intolerable, triggering a range of defensive moves." What is this phrase?

~~~

quiz question 3

DiAngelo beckons her fellow white people to their unjust marginalization. She says that their sensitivity is 'an obstacle to progress.' According to DiAngelo, who is her audience in the book?

quiz question 4

According to DiAngelo, there are two most
effective beliefs that prevent the white collective
from seeing that racism is a system. What are these
two beliefs?

quiz question 5

True or False: People who are born with mixed race may pass as white but will also experience a feeling of isolation and resentment from the people who cannot pass. Multiracial people may not ever be seen as "real" people of any color.

quiz question 6

True or False: Racial identity is assigned by people whose race is dominant in a certain community. For multiracial people, racial identity is further complicated by their parents' racial identity and the racial demographics of the community where they were raised.

~ ~ ~

quiz question 7

True or False: The most important of all is for whites to remember that they should shed their white fragility for the people of color. They should do it in the spirit of unity, honesty and truth.

~ ~ ~

quiz question 8

In college, Robin DiAngelo attended
_____. From here she earned
her bachelor's degree in History and Sociology. She
graduated Valedictorian of her class.

~ ~ ~

quiz question 9

In 2004, DiAngelo graduated with a Ph.D. in
_____ from
University of Washington. DiAngelo's doctoral
dissertation is entitled "Whiteness in racial
dialogue: a discourse analysis".

~~~

quiz question 10

In 2012, DiAngelo wrote *What Does it Mean to be White?: Developing White Racial Literacy.* This was followed by her book

_____

_____. This was published in 2017 as part of Multicultural Education Series.

~~~

~~~

quiz question 11

True or False: DiAngelo holds the distinction that she grew up poor and white. She says that her experience of poverty wouldn't have been different if she were not white.

~~~

~~~

quiz question 12

True or False: DiAngelo is widely known as the one who coined the term "white fragility". She first used the term in a peer-reviewed paper she write in 2011. This term was used in contrast to the jargon "people of color."

~~~

Quiz Answers

1. Passing
2. White Fragility
3. White Collective
4. That racists are bad people and that racism is conscious dislike
5. True
6. True
7. False
8. Seattle University
9. Critical Multicultural Education and Whiteness Studies
10. *Is Everyone Really Equal?: An Introduction to Key Concepts in Social Justice Education*
11. False
12. True

Ways to Continue Your Reading

E VERY month, our team runs through a wide selection of books to pick the best titles for readers and reading groups, and promotes these titles to our thousands of readers – sometimes with free downloads, sale dates, and additional brochures.

Click here to sign up for these benefits.

If you have not yet read the original work or would like to read it again, you can purchase the original book here.

Bonus Downloads
Get Free Books with __Any Purchase__ of Conversation Starters!

Every purchase comes with a FREE download!

Add spice to any conversation
Never run out of things to say
Spend time with those you love

Get it Now

or Click Here.

Scan Your Phone

On the Next Page...

If you found this book helpful to your discussions and rate it a 4 or 5, please write us a review on the next page.

Any length would be fine but we'd appreciate hearing you more! We'd be very encouraged.

Till next time,

BookHabits

"Loving Books is Actually a Habit"

CPSIA information can be obtained
at www.ICGtesting.com
Printed in the USA
LVHW040332010620
657104LV00002B/374